The Story of
JAMESTOWN

By Marilyn Prolman

Illustrated by Chuck Mitchell

CHILDRENS PRESS, CHICAGO

Library of Congress Catalog Card Number: 73-82963

4 5 6 7 8 9 10 11 12 13 14 15 16 17 18 19 20 21 22 23 24 25   R 75

Eighteen-year-old John Dods turned from his packing to answer the door.

"I've come to say farewell, my friend," said the tall, young man standing in the doorway. "I shall be hard at work when you leave tomorrow."

"Yes, tomorrow I sail for Virginia. When I board the *Susan Constant* in the morning I will begin a new life," replied John, as he stuffed a pair of pants into his bag.

"Won't you change your mind, John?" his friend asked. "It's a long and dangerous trip."

"I'm not afraid. Whatever troubles the New World may hold, I can survive them. Why don't you come with me?" asked John. "England holds nothing for either of us. If you are not a member of the nobility or a merchant, what will you have when you are old and can't work? Perhaps a little money, but no land to call your own. In Virginia, rich lands wait for men to claim them. Gold sits untouched in the ground. Precious gems lie on the beaches to be gathered by the basketful. Come with me and be rich, free, and happy in the New World."

Frowning, his friend replied, "I wish I could believe as you do, John. I wish you good fortune, though I admit I do not believe it awaits you. Good-bye, John."

Sunrise the next morning found John Dods walking along the wharf, looking at the three ships that were to sail to Virginia. The ships belonged to the London Company, a group of men who were paying for the colonization of Virginia. In return for the money they spent to send settlers there, they wanted to make great profits selling the goods from the New World in England, just as the East India Company had made money from the silks and spices of the Orient. But most of all, the London Company hoped that the colonists would find gold in Virginia.

"There's my ship, the *Susan Constant*," said John. "I see I've had good luck already. She seems to be larger and more seaworthy than either the *Godspeed* or the *Discovery*."

Some of the passengers were beginning to board the vessels. Because life in Virginia would be difficult at first, no women were sailing on the first voyage. They would come later.

Wanting to know who his traveling companions were, John stood and watched the passengers as they boarded the ships. He saw two laborers like himself boarding the *Godspeed*. But there were men who were richer than he, better dressed, and with more possessions. He had heard that gentlemen would go on the voyage, but he was surprised to see how many there really were. A well-dressed man stood near John waiting to go aboard.

"This man looks to be a gentleman and a friendly sort, I'll ask him why he and so many other rich men are going to Virginia," John thought.

"Are you going to the New World?" John asked the man.

"Yes, lad," he replied. The gentleman smiled and continued, "I may look like a rich man, but actually the British system offers me as little as it offers a workman like you. When my father dies, all his money, houses, and lands will go to my oldest brother. In England, the younger brother inherits nothing. To have any property or money, he has to depend on the generosity of his older brother, and if you think my brother would share with me, you're mistaken."

"I see," said John, thoughtfully, as the gentleman hurried toward his ship.

After boarding the *Susan Constant* and stowing away his baggage, John found that there were two goldsmiths, two gold refiners, and a jeweler among the passengers on board. He saw some farmers, but very few. "I should think the new land would need many farmers. The London Company may not care whether we eat, but it is certainly prepared to take care of any gold and jewels we find," thought John bitterly.

The ships were supposed to sail that December morning, but bad weather forced them to wait in the harbor for six weeks. Finally, in February of 1607, the weather cleared and the three, little ships set sail for the New World.

The unsuspecting passengers did not know what was in store for them. More bad weather hit the ships when they were out at sea. The ships were overcrowded and there was very little space to walk around. The men had nothing to eat but hard biscuits, heavily salted meat and fish, and thin, watery barley gruel. Most of the time, however, many of the passengers were too ill to eat.

Finally, early on the morning of April 26, the three vessels dropped anchor in a bay on the Virginia coast. All the passengers ran to the decks to get their first glimpse of the new land.

And what a land it was! From the ships they saw forests taller and thicker than any in England. The first men to go ashore found grapevines, raspberry bushes, and giant strawberry plants growing everywhere. There were traces of opossum, raccoon, deer, bear, beaver, and muskrat in the woods. Although no precious gems lay on the beaches, they did find shellfish. To men who had eaten only ship's food for several months, shellfish were as valuable as any gems.

That evening, several of the important gentlemen on the voyage and the captains of the ships assembled in the cabin of Christopher Newport, the captain of the *Susan Constant*. Captain Newport had been given complete command of the expedition since it left England. After the men were seated Captain Newport solemnly opened the sealed box that the London Company had given him.

"These are our instructions," he said. "First they tell us how to deal with the Indians and to choose a site for our settlement. They urge us to plant our crops right away so we will have food in the autumn. And, yes, we must search for gold and try to find traces of the Lost Colony of Roanoke. But most important, here are the names of the seven men the London Company has chosen for our new colony's governing council."

As Captain Newport read each name, the men nodded their heads in agreement. All three ships' captains had been chosen, as well as the most honored and respected gentlemen. However, when the seventh and last name was read, the captain of the *Discovery*, jumped to his feet in protest.

"John Smith!" he cried. "Why, that man is on board my ship in chains. He is an adventurer. During the entire journey, he criticized every decision I made. And I believe he was also planning a mutiny!"

All the men present began arguing over John

Smith's place on the council. Captain Newport called for order. "If the London Company saw fit to name him as one of the council members," he said, "then he shall be one." The men reluctantly agreed with Captain Newport.

John Smith was released and given his proper position on the council, but many still resented him.

The quarrel over seating John Smith on the council was only one of many that would plague the colony throughout its existence. A few days later, another quarrel began when the council members were choosing a permanent site for the settlement. The ships had sailed about thirty miles up the river and the councillors were considering a flat peninsula on the north bank.

"The river is deep enough here to moor the ships to the trees," said one councillor, "and there is a clear view all the way down the river. We can defend this spot easily."

"But the land is low and swampy," objected another. "And the sandy soil is poor for raising crops. We won't be able to grow enough food here."

"There are no brooks or springs to supply us with fresh drinking water," a third councillor added. "The river is salty at high tide, and when the tide goes out the river is full of muck. We can't settle here."

There was not enough time to look farther. Planting had to be done soon or they would have no food later. The majority of the councillors favored the spot so it was chosen.

On May 13, 1607, the colonists left the ships and brought their personal belongings ashore. Edward-Maria Wingfield, who had been elected president of the council, gathered the men around him. "I declare this site to be named Jamestown. The people who dwell herein will honor God and the great King James I of England." Tents were set up on the bank. For the first time, the men slept on the land they had journeyed so long to claim.

The next day John Smith called all the colonists together. "We must begin to build a fort as protection against the Indians. Everyone will help."

Realizing the need for a fort, work began immediately. But, everyone did not help. John Dods and the other laborers and craftsmen worked from sunrise to sunset, taking time out only to eat and pray. They cleared the land by cutting down trees and bushes. They fashioned the tree trunks into great tall poles. They dug trenches. They stood the poles up in the trenches to make high wooden walls.

But the gentlemen colonists refused to do any manual labor. In England, they had always had servants to do their work, and they saw no reason why things should be any different in Virginia. John Smith made many enemies by insisting that everyone do their share. Many gentlemen, however, still refused to do any but supervisory jobs.

The work on the fort continued. The busy colonists did not know that the Indians had been watching them for days. One morning, as the work went on as usual, a man suddenly cried out. Everyone stopped working and turned to see the man fall with an arrow in his back. While the men were working, the Indians had crept up taking the colonists completely by surprise. In the confusion that followed, a boy and twenty men were wounded before the settlers could begin to fight back.

"Get to the ship!" someone shouted.

Several men ran to the ship, which was moored nearby. They fired the ship's cannon. Frightened by the booming gun, the Indians fled into the forest.

After the attack, the colonists realized how much they needed a fort for protection. Everyone worked. Soon it was finished. The fort was triangular, 420 feet long on the side facing the river, 300 feet long on the other two sides. Cannon were mounted at the corners. Strong walls enclosed about one acre of ground.

Here, safe inside the walls, the settlers pitched their tents. With the fort completed, the colonists assembled in their makeshift church, made of a sail stretched across two trees. They received communion and prayed that the new land would bring them prosperity. Unfortunately, this prayer would not be answered for a long time. Supplies were running low. More tools and food were needed if work was to continue.

The next day Captain Newport sailed for England. He carried with him some ore samples. If he found gold, the London Company would be satisfied.

While Captain Newport was in England, conditions in the colony continually grew worse. Few provisions were left. In the heat of summer much of the food spoiled. Having no fresh water supply, the men were forced to drink the murky water of the river and illness swept through the fort. Malaria mosquitoes that bred in a nearby swamp infected many of the people. The land that had been so hastily chosen by the councillors was almost uninhabitable. By December of 1607 only about fifty colonists were left, and these were on the verge of starvation.

The leaders began quarreling among themselves. Each one had a different solution to their problem. The fights resolved nothing. Finally, John Smith took over. He and two other men went in search of food.

Since the James River and most of the country near the settlement had been explored, Smith decided to sail up the unexplored Chickahominy River ten miles upriver from Jamestown.

The river grew narrower and narrower, the farther they went. When travel by boat became impossible, Smith decided to go on by foot. Leaving the two men to guard the boat and wait for his return, he set off through the forest. Smith searched for game and berries but found very little. He had decided to turn back when, suddenly, the Indians attacked. Fighting bravely, Smith killed two Indians. But far outnumbered by the Indians, he was taken prisoner.

The Indians took him to their chief. The chief eyed the prisoner carefully, then, as he had imagined, sentenced him to death. But John Smith did not quietly accept his fate. He pulled his compass from his pocket and showed it to the Indians. Then he began to talk. Although they could not understand a word he said, the Indians listened. They looked closely at his marvelous "magical" compass, watching the needle which always pointed to Captain Smith. Thinking he was some sort of god, the Indians took him to the village of the chief of the whole region, Powhatan.

Powhatan was not impressed by Smith's magic. He sentenced Smith to death for murdering two Indians. Smith was to be killed in the Indian way. He would be clubbed to death by the Indian braves.

Preparations were made for the execution. Braves brought rocks and piled them in a low mound in the center of the village. All the inhabitants of the village formed a large circle. Then, John was brought in and laid down, his head resting on the rock mound. The Indian braves surrounded John and raised their clubs.

Suddenly Powhatan's twelve-year-old daughter, Pocahontas, ran out of the crowd. She lay her head next to Smith's and begged her father not to kill him. Chief Powhatan let his favorite daughter have her way. He spared John Smith's life.

When John Smith returned to Jamestown, he brought with him a promise of peace with the Indians and a boatload of Indian corn. But to his amazement no welcome awaited him. His enemies now controlled the council. They denounced him, claiming he was responsible for the deaths of the two men who had scouted with him. They arrested him, tried him for murder, and found him guilty. Once again John Smith was sentenced to death!

On the day set for the hanging, Captain Newport's ship sailed into the James River. Upon hearing of John Smith's death sentence, Newport rushed to the council. Overriding their objections, Captain Newport granted Smith his freedom. For the third time John Smith's life had been saved.

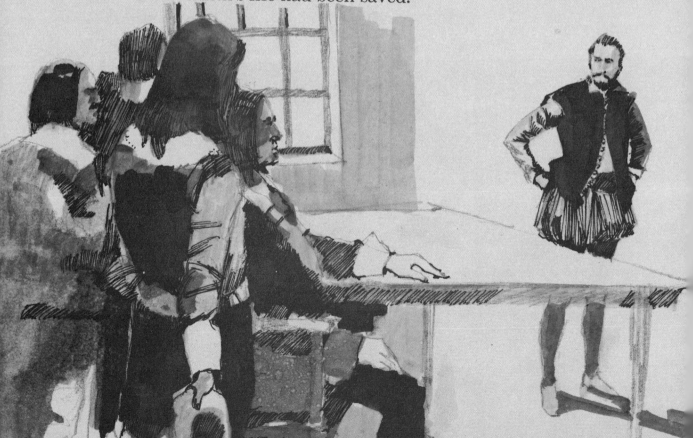

Captain Newport stayed in Jamestown only long enough to unload his cargo of food and arms, and the new settlers. He reported that the ore he had taken to England was worthless. It was iron pyrites, or "fool's gold." Then once again he set sail for England.

John Smith soon was elected president of the council. He proved to be one of Jamestown's few practical leaders. He insisted that the colonists think of the future. Under his leadership, the settlers began to clear the fields, plant corn, put up small huts, and build a blockhouse to defend the Jamestown peninsula. Smith brought a few hogs out to an island and left them there to breed and roam free. In eighteen months Hog Island had a population of more than sixty pigs. A few chickens, left free the same way, soon numbered five hundred.

Although he did a great deal for the colony, Smith was not always appreciated. His enemies constantly looked for an excuse to send him back to England. At last they found one. Smith received a gunpowder wound in his thigh. His enemies, pretending to be concerned, insisted that he return to England.

John Smith never returned to his beloved Virginia. He had been in the New World only two years, but he had done much for the struggling colony. By the time he left, the colonists had a glassworks, twenty houses, a church, and a well pumping clean water. They were shipping cargoes of glass, pitch, and iron ore to England. But the London Company was not satisfied. It still asked for gold.

In time the men of the London Company realized there was no gold in Virginia. They also thought that the ever-squabbling council was not fit to govern. So they appointed Thomas West, Lord De la Warr, the first all-powerful governor in the colony.

The month before John Smith was sent back to England, seven, hurricane-battered ships carrying this news arrived in Jamestown. On the ships were nearly three hundred passengers, most of them ill or dying. Nine ships had started out on the journey, but one had sunk and another was reported down off Bermuda. Aboard that ship was the new lieutenant governor, Thomas Gates. He was presumed dead until one day, nine months later, two small ships sailed into the harbor at Jamestown. Gates got off one of the ships and told a strange tale.

"Our ship, the *Sea Venture*, went down off Bermuda," he said. "Fortunately land was near. We could not save our ship, but we did save ourselves. We swam ashore. Not a single life was lost.

"The Bermuda climate was delightful. We ate fruit and the fish and shellfish we could get from the sea. We salvaged what timbers we could from the *Sea Venture* and built the crafts you see here. Then we put out to sea. Our crafts proved seaworthy, and here we are."

The colonists also had a tale to tell, and one with a less happy ending. A very thin John Dods stepped forward and told the new colonists, "This winter we lost most of our population. There were five hundred of us when John Smith left. Now there are sixty-five.

"First, thirty men went to barter with the Indians for food. In the midst of the talks, they were massacred. Then one by one the people here began to starve to death. We buried them without ceremony in huge common graves.

"When all our food was gone we lived for awhile on horsemeat. Soon that, too, was gone. We ate dogs and cats. The we ate rats and mice. We ate anything we pulled up in our fishing nets, and there was not much. We chewed leather. And still the men died—three, four, five, ten men a day. Those who were strong enough killed snakes and ate them. We ate all kinds of roots. And still the men died. You look now upon all that is left of the colony."

The new arrivals were shocked. They took the starving men aboard their ships and planned to sail at once for England.

Just then a ship was sighted coming up the river. It carried provisions and the new governor, Lord De la Warr. If the ship had not appeared just then, the colony of Virginia probably would have been abandoned.

Life went on in the colony. The settlers tried to

find a crop that they could export to England to satisfy the London Company. But none of their attempts succeeded.

Then John Rolfe, who had come with Lieutenant Governor Gates, began to experiment with the native tobacco weed. The Indians smoked it, but it was too strong and bitter for European tastes. Rolfe got some West Indies tobacco and had good luck growing it in the Virginia soil. In 1613 he sent his first boatload of tobacco to England.

King James called it loathsome to the eye, hateful to the nose, harmful to the brain, and dangerous to the lungs. The public, however, loved it. In 1615, 2300 pounds of tobacco were sent to England. Two years later 20,000 pounds were sent. The colony had found its first profitable export product.

John Rolfe prospered along with the colony. He married Pocahontas, the Indian girl who had saved John Smith's life. She had been converted to Christianity and baptized with the name Rebecca. Powhatan approved of the marriage. But he still did not trust white men and refused to visit the white settlement. A few years later Rolfe took his wife and their infant son to visit England. There Lady Rebecca saw again her old friend John Smith. Several months later, just when Rolfe was to take her back to Jamestown, she became ill. Within a few days she was dead of smallpox.

Rolfe returned to the colony. Tobacco grew everywhere. It was used as money in the colony. The value of products was determined in pounds of tobacco. The leaf supported more and more colonists. In 1619 alone, more than one thousand new colonists arrived. Among the new colonists was a shipload of young women. The London Company thought that if the colonists had wives and families they would stay permanently in Virginia.

The Jamestown settlement was expanding. Plan-

tations and farms stretched along the tidewater rivers. The colonists set up the first American legislature in 1619. There was a general assembly consisting of twenty-two burgesses, a governor, and six councillors. The assembly, called the House of Burgess, passed laws to make the colony self-sufficient. Each landowner was required to plant ten wild grapevines for wine, one hundred flax plants for linen, and six mulberry trees to feed the silkworms for a silk industry.

The colony seemed to be thriving. The settlers had enough to eat. There was a cash crop to export to England and relative peace with the Indians.

Then suddenly, on Good Friday, 1622, the Indians attacked the widespread plantations. By the end of the day, 350 colonists had been massacred. John Rolfe and several of the councillors were among the dead.

Fortunately, the people of Jamestown had been warned and were able to defend the town.

The surviving settlers moved into the town. Living conditions were crowded and unsanitary. A plague broke out, spread through the town, and killed another seven hundred persons. The future of Jamestown looked bleak.

Events in England made the situation even worse. The London Company had been dissolved. The king was now going to rule Virginia. He was jealous of the freedom the colony had, so the first thing he did was to abolish the democratic general assembly. The people of the colony groaned when they heard the news.

"Life here gets worse and worse," they said. "First the climate tried to kill us, then the Indians. Now the king has taken away the few rights and privileges that made our life worth living."

Nevertheless an era of prosperity followed. The colonists began to expand along the James and York rivers. Their new houses were of brick and wood, built to last. Some were built as row houses. Others were single residences. Jamestown began to have an air of permanence about it.

By 1625 only three men from the first three ships still lived in the colony. They had lived through the Indian attack on the fort, the first hot summer, the starving time of 1607-1610, the massacre of 1622, and the plague of 1623. All had prospered. One of the three

was John Dods. He and his wife Jane had 50 acres of land in Jamestown and 150 acres across the river near Charles City, where they lived.

Virginians in general were pleased with the rule of Governor Wyatt, who restored the general assembly. He was followed in 1643 by Sir William Berkelely, who repealed a hated poll tax, made peace with colonists in the Chesapeake Bay area, and talked of sending expeditions to explore the West. But Berkeley's term of office was not to remain peaceful.

The Indians led another massacre against the colony.

In England, in 1649, Oliver Cromwell and the Parliament took control of the government. England was no longer ruled by a king. Cromwell sent his men to rule Virginia. Berkeley, a king's man, was forced to retire. Under Cromwell's rule, Virginia continued to prosper. It became more democratic.

Then the death of Cromwell and the return of Berkeley as royal governor ushered in a less favorable era. Berkeley was different. He brought back the tax laws and overruled many of the colony's democratic measures. He favored the interests of rich planters and merchants, rather than those of the small farmers who had come to Virginia to build new lives. Also, a drop in the price of tobacco brought real hardship.

At that time there was a young planter named

Nathaniel Bacon who did not care for Berkeley's rule. He also felt that Berkeley did not defend the western frontier against the Indians. When Indians attacked several plantations including his own, Bacon called together other planters who had suffered losses in the Indian raids. The men rallied around Bacon to fight Governor Berkeley.

The battle between Berkeley and Bacon became the first American revolution. Bacon in urging the people to fight for their liberties or leave the colony may have helped prepare Virginians to sign the Declaration of Independence more than a hundred years later.

Royal governors came and went. The colony grew. The frontier moved westward. Williamsburg became the capital of Virginia. Jamestown, the first permanent colony in America, was abandoned but not forgotten.

Not a single building of the Jamestown settlement stands today. But the reconstruction of Jamestown makes it a popular tourist site. Every year thousands of school children make the trip to Jamestown where they tour the quaint rustic houses, general stores, and churches with Indian guides. They see Jamestown as it was, an outpost in the wilderness where men battled climate, hunger, hostile Indians, disease, and injustice as they helped establish the principles upon which a great nation would be founded.

About the Author: Marilyn Prolman was born in Boston, Massachusetts. She attended the University of Wisconsin where she majored in English. She is a free-lance writer and has written several books for young readers. A mid-westerner by choice, she has lived in Chicago since her graduation.

About the Artist: Chuck Mitchell presents a creative new approach to editorial illustration. He has, through his intensive research and unusual artistic approach avoided all stereotypes. His valid portraits effectively convey the unique atmosphere of each historical period. Intensely evident is the character of each man and woman whose individual acts combined to make history.